The Pentland Hills

Kenneth R Bogle & Susan Falconer

This 1930s postcard shows the familiar outline of the Pentland Hills from Leadburn.

Text © Kenneth R Bogle & Susan Falconer, 2010.
First published in the United Kingdom, 2010,
by Stenlake Publishing Ltd.
Telephone: 01290 551122
www.stenlake.co.uk

ISBN 9781840335255

**The publishers regret that they cannot supply
copies of any pictures featured in this book.**

Acknowledgements

The authors and publisher wish to thank the following people who helped us with this book: Sybil Cavanagh, Catriona Davies, Michael Jones, George Kemp, Alan McLaren, Anne Morrison, Katherine Morgan, Neil 'Drouthy' MacVicar, Alan Reid, Alan Cameron and the old boys at West Linton, Ron Sheridan and the coffee drinkers at Penicuik, and Pia Simig and the good folk at Little Sparta. Special thanks to Alison Bogle for having to tramp around the hills with bundles of old photographs and also to the Friends of the Pentlands who helped to spread the word about our project. The authors and publishers would like to thank the following for contributing photographs for this book: Edinburgh City Libraries for the front cover and pages 11 (larger) and 13; Alan McLaren for the inside front cover; Michael Jones for page 6; *The Scotsman* Publications Limited for pages 15 (larger), 20, 22, 46 (larger), 55 and the inside back cover; George Kemp for pages 19, 38, 50, 52 and 53; *The Advertiser* for page 21; Penicuik Historical Society for page 35; West Linton and District Historical Association for pages 41, 43, 47 and 48; the Scottish Rights of Way Society for page 49; the estate of Ian Hamilton Finlay for page 54 (larger); and West Lothian Local History Library and West Lothian History Society for page 54 (smaller). All of the other images are from the collection of Midlothian Library Service Local Studies, Loanhead. The authors have made every effort to contact copyright holders and we apologise if we have unwittingly infringed copyright.

Further reading

Now that you *own* this book you don't really need any others, of course, but there is a rich literature about the Pentland Hills that, like the Hills themselves, is well worth exploring. Anybody interested in the Pentlands will soon discover Will Grant. His books *The Call of the Pentlands* (Robert Grant & Son, 1927: second edition, Oliver & Boyd, 1951) and *Pentland Days and Country Ways* (Nelsons, 1934) are the bibles of Pentland study and are unlikely to be surpassed. Earlier books include Robert Cochrane *Pentland Walks with their Literary and Historical Associations* (Andrew Elliot, 1908), George M Reith *The Breezy Pentlands* (TN Foulis, 1910) and William Anderson *The Pentland Hills* (Chambers, 1926). More recent is Jim Crumley *Discovering the Pentland Hills* (John Donald, 1991). The best modern guide for walkers is Susan Falconer *The Pentland Hills: a Walker's Guide* (Cicerone, 2007). There are many books about the towns and villages around the Pentlands and the hills are mentioned in general accounts of Scottish geology, landscape, literature and history, both human and natural.

Introduction

Describing the journey from Liberton to Melville Castle one day in November 1827, Sir Walter Scott wrote in his journal: 'I think I never saw anything more beautiful than the ridge of Carnethy against a clear, frosty sky, with its peaks and varied slopes. The hills glowed like purple amethysts, the sky glowed topaz and vermilion colours. I never saw a finer screen than Pentland, considering that it is neither rocky nor highly elevated.' The Pentland Hills have long attracted this kind of affection. They are amongst the best loved hills in Scotland and have been admired by generations of walkers, tourists, writers, artists, lovers of nature and those who just happen to live near them, even if they have not actually visited them. In the words of Robert Louis Stevenson, who was one of their greatest devotees, they are the hills of home.

The Pentlands cover an area of approximately 75 square miles, running south-west from Edinburgh in a series of switchback ridges before gently falling away to moorland in the west. The Pentlands are not especially high (until, that is, you start to climb one) and they are dwarfed by the Highland mountains further north. They reach their greatest elevation at Scald Law which is 1899 feet above sea level. The distinctive shape of the hills was created eons ago by the relentless movement of glaciers and melt-water. Today they are principally covered in grass and heather with occasional rocky outcrops.

The name Pentland is thought to come from the settlement of Pentland at the eastern end of the hills, a few miles north of Penicuik. One group of early settlers in the Lothians spoke Cumbric, the ancestor of modern Welsh. Pentland probably comes from their *pen llan* meaning 'the height above the enclosed land or church'. An ancient burial ground still stands at the site of Old Pentland Church which in turn was somewhere near to the original settlement. Early maps of the Pentlands show a singular Pentland Hill in the north of the hills and this might have been the area where cattle from Pentland village were taken to graze in the summer. The likeliest explanation is that the name Pentland spread from the original settlement to the hill and then to the entire range.

There is a long history of human activity in the Pentlands and people have always used the natural resources that the hills provide. The earliest settlers left behind them many archaeological remains whose functions we can now only guess at. Several prominent summits have ancient stone cairns on top of them, such as the huge rocky cairn on Carnethy Hill, the second highest peak in the Pentlands. There are traces of ancient forts, settlements and earthworks all over the hills, the most impressive of which is the great Iron Age hill fort and souterrain (an underground chamber or passage) at Castlelaw. Down the road near Glencorse Church there is a fine example of a cup-and-ring-marked stone, enigmatic and forever unknowable. No doubt many other ancient sites have disappeared over time. In 1843 the *New Statistical Account* recorded a stone circle or 'Druidical temple' at Marchwell Farm near Penicuik but this has since been lost. The Romans knew about the Pentlands; the modern A702 road between Edinburgh and Biggar largely follows the course of an old Roman road. Fragments of Roman pottery and other artefacts have been found in the hills. It is, of course, impossible to know what these early people thought about the hills above and around them. Most likely they had little time for the Romantic idea that wild landscapes are places of beauty and contemplation, somewhere to connect with nature and cleanse the soul. Rather the hills were part of a harsh and unpredictable environment from which they had to eke out some kind of existence. But it would also be nice to think that sometimes on a sunny evening when their work was done they looked up at the hills and felt content.

Later periods of history have also left their mark on the Pentlands. There are old tower houses and churches around the base of the hills, many now in ruins but some still in use. Occasionally in dry spells the remains of the drowned medieval chapel of St. Katherine's-in-the-Hopes re-emerges from the waters of Glencorse Reservoir. Modern walkers can still follow the route that the monks used from the lost monastery at Newhall on their way to the sea, passing the remains of an ancient stone cross to guide them. There are many old roads, tracks and passes through the hills, some of which were once used by cattle drovers going to southern markets. The Pentlands have strong associations with the radical Covenanters of the seventeenth-century. The hills have plenty of secluded places for secret worship and in 1666 there was a major battle between the Covenanters and Government forces at Rullion Green. There can be few more evocative sites in the whole of Scotland than the lonely Covenanter's Grave near the summit of Black Law.

The growth of towns and rise of industries in the Lothians such as paper-making and mining led to an insatiable demand for fresh water. Ambitious engineering projects created the various Pentland reservoirs that we see today, such as Glencorse, Loganlea and Baddinsgill. The nineteenth century also saw huge improvements in transport and leisure. The first guidebook for ramblers was published in 1885, and bus and charabanc tours around and into the hills became available for the less active. Golf courses were built on the slopes of the hills near Edinburgh and at West Linton, and in the mid-1960s an artificial ski-slope was opened at Hillend. The Pentlands stage the annual Carnethy Five Hill Race and they have become a popular venue for mountain biking and other adventure sports.

There has been a military presence in the Pentlands ever since the Roman armies tramped their way through them. There are modern bases at Dreghorn and Glencorse and the army make use of the hills for training and exercises as well as the firing ranges at Castlelaw. At the same time, the Pentlands are working hills and provide a livelihood for local farmers and landowners. There are numerous farms scattered around the hills, sheep and cattle graze on the better land and large parts of heather moorland are burnt to encourage grouse. All of this activity has created great pressure on the hills and there has been some friction between different groups of users. In 1986 around half of the Pentlands range was designated as a Regional Park in an attempt to protect and conserve the character of the hills. Today the Pentland Hills Ranger Service works to protect and enhance the area, and to encourage visitors to act responsibly and with respect for others.

The Pentlands have a fine literary and artistic heritage, and some of the greatest Scottish writers have been inspired by them. Allan Ramsay immortalised the area around Carlops in his pastoral drama *The Gentle Shepherd*, and Scott and Stevenson were both enamoured of the hills. Others have also been caught in their spell, such as Will Ogilvie, the author of *In Pentland Wine*, one of the best poems about the hills. At Little Sparta near Dunsyre, the artist Ian Hamilton Finlay created a unique and wonderful garden where concrete poetry and sculpture have been merged into the natural landscape.

The modern Pentlands provide a wide variety of habitats for wildlife. The reservoirs are important places for wintering wildfowl such as pink-footed geese and whooper swans. Heather moorland supports the iconic red grouse and also mountain hares, emperor moths and green hairstreak butterflies. Grasslands are home to a variety of wildflowers such as harebell and ragged robin as well as brown hares, short-eared owls and ringlet butterflies. The Pentlands are not thickly wooded but they do have conifer plantations and the remnants of shelterbelts and plantings around the reservoirs. These are habitats for crossbills and sparrowhawks, and also for several species of bats. Raised bog such as Red Moss is home to many specially-adapted plants and animals that thrive in wet, acidic places.

This book tries to capture some of the history and character of the Pentland Hills through a series of old photographs and postcards. These have been chosen on artistic merit but we have tried to give as wide a spread as possible to show some of the major features of the hills. The book starts at Edinburgh and the eastern end of the hills, round to Glencorse and the valley of the Logan Burn, and then back out to the southern hills and finishing off in West Lothian. We hope that you enjoy the journey, that you will be encouraged to make some of your own and that you will come to love the hills as we do. All aboard.

Left: Edinburgh's hills. This engraving of the Pentlands from Duddingston Loch is one of the earliest known images of the hills. It was published in 1829 by Thomas H Shepherd in his book *Modern Athens*, which set out to exhibit 'the whole of the New Buildings, Modern Improvements, Antiquities and Picturesque Scenery of the Scottish Metropolis and Its Environs'. The artist has used some poetic licence but the basic outline of the hills is recognisable.

With its stony slopes, Caerketton Hill gives superb views over Edinburgh and into Fife and beyond. There are the remains of a prehistoric fort near the summit which probably gave the hill its name: *Caer* is a Cumbric name for fort, possibly of the refuge or the retreat.

This photograph shows the Edinburgh Mounted Special Constables on parade at Dreghorn, possibly in the early 1930s. The special constabulary was formed in December 1914 to augment the regular police force, many of whom had left to join the army. This included a mounted section which was composed of men over military age who were skilled riders and who owned a horse. Many were members of the local hunt. They carried out cavalry manoeuvres at the weekends and are shown here wearing their ceremonial uniforms with their distinctive spiked helmets. In the background are Allermuir and Capelaw Hills.

The picturesque village of Swanston nestles at the foot of Caerketton Hill and provides an ideal access point to the northern hills. Swanston was first recorded in the early thirteenth century although the name has a Norse derivation. The white-washed thatched cottages were built for estate workers in the eighteenth century. They had earth floors and were without running water or electricity well within living memory.

Along with Allan Ramsay, Robert Louis Stevenson is the greatest literary figure associated with the Pentland Hills. In the 1860s, Thomas Stevenson, Robert's father, rented Swanston Cottage as a summer retreat and it became the inspiration for many of RLS's poems and stories. John Tod, the 'Roaring Shepherd', was a great influence on the young Stevenson and encouraged him to love the hills, as RLS recalled in his collection *Memories and Portraits*. This postcard from 1908 shows the Roaring Shepherd's cottage at Swanston.

Kyling the Hay

This postcard shows 'Kyling the hay' at Swanston in the early 1920s. The farm worker and his boy with a Clydedale horse are gathering the hay into 'stooks' to allow it to dry. In the background are the scree-eroded slopes of Caerketton Hill.

Close to the northern end of the Pentlands, Bonaly Tower was constructed by Lord Henry Cockburn in the 1830s on the sight of an older farmhouse. Cockburn had a successful legal and literary career and was a well-known character in Edinburgh. He loved to roam the hills and wrote in his book *Memorials of His Time*: 'There is not a recess in the valleys of the Pentlands, nor an eminence on their summits, that is not familiar to my solitude.'

THE UPPER WATERFALL, TORDUFF, THE PENTLANDS.
98149.J.V.

Lying in a deep hollow and with fine views to Edinburgh, Torduff Reservoir was constructed in the late 1840s to gather water from the North Pentland Aqueduct. The larger photograph is taken from an engineer's photograph album dating from the 1880s. The road around the reservoir leads to a picturesque miniature waterfall before climbing to the level of Clubbiedean Reservoir.

Like its neighbour Torduff, Clubbiedean Reservoir (above) is a good place to see waterbirds. There are the remains of an Iron Age settlement at its western end. Further south-west, Threipmuir Reservoir is also an important site for wildlife. The name Threipmuir derives from the Scots 'Threpe' meaning debatable. In the past, local estates have argued about the ownership of this area. The reservoir is not used to provide water for Edinburgh but instead as a 'compensation supply' for the Water of Leith.

On the eastern side of Caerketton Hill, the Midlothian Snowsports Centre, formerly the Hillend Ski Centre was opened in October 1966 and is the longest dry ski run in Scotland. The centre provides skiing and snow-boarding all year round thanks to its artificial matting and floodlights. Many Scottish contestants in the Winter Olympic Games have been trained here.

Situated on the slopes of Woodhouselee Hill at the eastern end of the Pentlands, Woodhouselee House was built by the Tytler family at the end of the eighteenth century on the site of an old tower, parts of which were incorporated into the new mansion. The Tytlers were a prominent literary family and Woodhouselee had many important visitors, including Sir Walter Scott who helped to perpetuate several ghost stories about the house. George Meikle Kemp, the architect of the Scott Monument, designed a wing in 1843. The house and estate were sold in the 1930s and the house was demolished in 1965.

Glencorse Old Kirk is one of many intriguing churches that nestle in the foot of the Pentlands. It has been a religious site for many centuries and was much admired by Robert Louis Stevenson who attended regularly. The church fell into disrepair in the 1880s, as can be seen in this photograph from 1957, but recently it has been restored and can be hired for weddings and other events. The other photograph shows an old gravestone at Glencorse made out of a school writing slate. The story goes that James Henderson, the grieving father, was unable to afford a proper stone for his infant daughter Catherine. Stevenson described it as 'the most pathetic memorial I ever saw'. The original stone has been lost but there is a copy in New Glencorse Church.

Just north of Glencorse Church and affording fine views to the Pentlands there once stood this curious wooden footbridge over the Glencorse Burn. It was known as the Minister's Bridge because it gave access from the local manse to the church. Robert Louis Stevenson loved this spot and wrote about it with great fondness when he was exiled in Samoa. He asked his friend and fellow author SR Crockett to say a prayer for him there and promised that his ghost would appear in response.

THE FORD TO GLENCORSE OLD CHURCH.

JRR·E

The ford over the Glencorse Burn was notoriously difficult to cross, as this Edwardian lady cyclist has discovered, but there was a public outcry when the bridge and ford were eventually replaced in the early 1900s.

 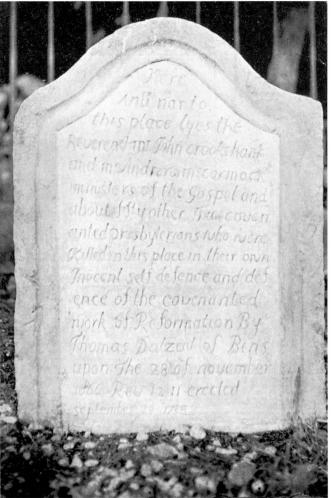

The Battle of Rullion Green was fought on 28th November 1666 between a Government army under the command of the infamous General Tam Dalziel of the Binns against a small band of Presbyterian Covenanters, who had marched on Edinburgh from the south west. The traditional site of the battle was on the eastern slopes of Turnhouse Hill where this monument was erected in 1738. Recently it has been suggested that the battle took place a little further to the north.

Rullion Green was a crushing defeat for the ill-equipped Covenanters, many of whom were killed or imprisoned, and fugitives from the battle tried to escape through the Pentland Hills. One of these was John Carphin, who although badly wounded made it as far as Adam Sanderson's cottage at Blackhall on the Medwin Water, about ten miles away. Carphin died of his wounds but the kindly shepherd buried him on the summit of Black Law within sight of his Ayrshire home. The stone at the Covenanter's Grave was erected in 1841.

Following the re-establishment of the Crown's control of the Church of Scotland in the 1660s, many Presbyterian ministers were ousted from their parishes and forced to hold illegal assemblies in the open air or farm buildings. The memory of these Conventicles continued well into the twentieth century, including regular meetings in the Pentland Hills. Taken in June 1958, this photograph shows Dr DGD Isaac addressing the St. Giles Cathedral Fellowship on the slopes of Castlelaw Hill. Glencorse Reservoir is in the background.

Carnethy Five Hills Race commemorates the battle of Roslin, which was fought in the Midlothian area in February 1302 as part of the Scottish Wars of Independence. The first Carnethy Race was held on 27th February 1971. The entry fee was 2/- which included a meal. The route of the race has changed several times since then and is now a six mile run with 2,500 feet of ascent across five summits. This photograph shows competitors in the snow during the 1990 race.

This aerial view shows Glencorse Reservoir in the heart of the northern hills, which was built between 1819 and 1822 to supply fresh water to Edinburgh and as a compensation pond for the mills along the River North Esk. There has always been a great demand for water in Edinburgh and after a series of dry summers in the early 1800s the Edinburgh Water Company was formed to develop the Glencorse site. The reservoir was designed by the great Scottish civil engineer Thomas Telford and the work was supervised by James Jardine. The construction employed 300 men for three years and cost £209,000 to complete.

The popular and picturesque road through the northern Pentlands winds around the top of Glencorse Reservoir and into the valley of the Logan Burn. This photograph shows Glencorse during a very dry spell sometime around 1900. The smaller photograph shows the remains of the medieval chapel of St. Katherine's-in-the-Hopes, which was submerged when the new reservoir was built. Occasionally the chapel resurfaces when the reservoir levels fall, as shown in this picture from 1933.

Kirkton Farmhouse in the Logan Valley is one of several isolated farms in the Pentlands. Turnhouse Hill and Carnethy Hill are in the background.

This photograph was one of many taken before the First World War by the Bryce family of Roslin and later turned into a hand-coloured postcard, which was sold to walkers and day-trippers. It is looking north east down the Logan Burn to Castlelaw Hill.

LOGANLEE COTTAGE, THE PENTLAND HILLS.   98152.

In the heart of the northern hills, the old water worker's cottage at the head of Loganlee Reservoir once did an enterprising sideline in pots of tea and bread and butter for hungry walkers. In the background are Turnhouse and Castlelaw Hills.

After a series of droughts in Edinburgh, Loganlee Reservoir was built between 1847 and 1851 by the Edinburgh Water Company to supply water to the city. The well-constructed road on the side of the reservoir was perfect for coach trips going to the head of the valley.

PRESBYTERY RUINS, ST. KATHERINE'S CHAPEL, THE PENTLANDS

On the northern slopes of Loganlee Reservoir there are the ruins of Howlet's House ('Owl's House'). This might have been the priest's house for St. Katherine's Chapel further down the glen or some kind of hostelry for cattle drovers and travellers.

This lovely atmospheric photograph taken around 1905 shows the Logan Valley looking north east. Loganlee Reservoir nestles under the slopes of Carnethy Hill and Scald Law on the right and the scree-strewn sides of Black Hill on the left. The ruined shepherd's cottage at the head of the reservoir is called The Howe and has since been rebuilt.

The large grassy area at the end of the Logan Valley was perfect for outings and Sunday School picnics. This photograph is believed to show the Loanhead South United Free Church Sunday School picnic in July 1901. The local newspaper reported that thirty vehicles were used to convey everybody and goes on: 'A pleasant day was spent, but the return home was greatly marred by wet.'

Left: The East and West Kips are very distinctively shaped hills, the name coming from the Scots meaning a sharp-pointed hill. This picture shows East Kip from the Logan Burn.

Right: Carnethy Hill, shown here from the valley of Green Cleugh, is the second highest in the Pentlands range, just beaten by its neighbour Scald Law. The name is probably derived from the Welsh *carneddau*, meaning rocky heaps. The summit has an enormous stone cairn which has been dated to the early Bronze Age.

THE VALLEY of the LOGAN BURN

S-531

These photographs show two sites in the Pentlands that are of great interest to modern naturalists. The glacial channel at Green Cleugh, described here as the Valley of the Logan Burn, was formed at the end of the Ice Age when remnants of glaciers forged a steep-sided cleft between Hare Hill and Black Hill. The other photograph was taken around 1900 and shows the Bryce family of Roslin, who took some of the other pictures in this book, enjoying a visit to the picturesque waterfall at the head of the Logan Valley. This has now been designated a Site of Special Scientific Interest for its rare, lime-loving plants.

383.

Penicuik from Uttershill Castle

The name Penicuik means 'the place of the cuckoo' which indicates the town's pastoral origins. The Pentland Hills are close at hand and can be seen from many places in the town. The ruined tower at Uttershill high above Penicuik provides a fine panorama of the hills.

The manufacture of paper began in Penicuik in the early eighteenth century and the town became famous for its high quality paper products. Manufacturers were drawn to the area because of the abundance of clear strong-running water from the Pentland Hills, used to drive machinery and in the papermaking process. The biggest of all the Penicuik mills was at Valleyfield, shown in this postcard with the Pentlands in the background.

This postcard from the mid 1920s shows a group of workers from Esk Mills paper factory at Penicuik enjoying a picnic at North Esk Reservoir in the Pentlands.

The hamlet of Silverburn nestles at the foot of Scald Law, the highest hill in the Pentlands. Some writers have suggested that Scald Law means the poet's or bard's hill but more likely the name comes from the Scots for scrabbled or patchy hill, referring to the scree slopes on the hill's eastern side. For many years there was a blacksmith's forge here which, amongst other items, made new shoes for horses using the busy road between Edinburgh and Biggar.

Nine Mile Burn near Carlops is nine Scots miles from Edinburgh. It was once famous for its blacksmith's smiddy and a popular Scottish song *Robin Tamson's Smiddy* written in the 1820s by Alexander Rodger. The thatched cottage in the postcard was demolished around 1910. George Meikle Kemp, the architect of the Scott Monument in Princes Street Gardens, Edinburgh, was brought-up nearby.

The Monks Road is an old track from Nine Mile Burn that leads onto Monks Rig and through the hills. It has been suggested that there was once a monastery at Newhall and the monks used this route to reach Edinburgh and beyond. However no trace of the monastery has been found and the name might be a corruption of St. Mungo. Near the crest of the hill is the Font Stone which was the base socket of an ancient stone cross. Crosses of this kind were used to mark pilgrimage routes and roads. The ornamental top of the cross was still in existence in the early nineteenth century but has now disappeared. Here two pupils from Penicuik High School, dressed in their regulation Midlothian Council cagoules, examine the Font Stone.

Newhall House near Carlops was rebuilt in the early eighteenth century by Sir David Forbes, a prominent Edinburgh lawyer. The house became a favourite haunt of prominent literary figures, including the Scottish poet and dramatist Allan Ramsay who set his pastoral comedy *The Gentle Shepherd* in the local area. The play was published in 1725 and describes rustic life and courtship amongst the Pentland Hills.

Allan Ramsay is commemorated on a memorial obelisk at Ravensneuk near Penicuik which looks onto his beloved Pentland hills.

Allan Ramsay's *The Gentle Shepherd* is now largely forgotten and is rarely performed but it was a minor literary sensation in its day, including an opera version. The success of Ramsay's play meant that the area around Carlops became a popular destination for tourists and day-trippers, such as this Edwardian group dancing in the picturesque wooded dell at Habbie's Howe.

Fresh air, countryside and, perhaps, some sensible romance as these Edwardian visitors, who do not look dressed for the Pentlands, explore the riverside at Habbie's Howe.

The Allan Ramsay Hotel at Carlops was built in 1792 to cater for visitors and is still one of the most welcoming howfs in the Pentlands area.

The tiny village of Carlops nestles at the foot of the Pentlands just inside the county boundary of Peeblesshire (now part of the Scottish Borders). Carlops can be traced back to the fourteenth century but the village really dates from the 1780s when there was an attempt to establish a local weaving industry. Later Carlops became popular with visitors as a base to walk the hills and explore the local scenery.

The church at Carlops was built in 1850 originally as the Free Church but in 1929 it joined with the Church of Scotland.

North Esk River Pentland Hills.   Carlops.

2065. Albany Series.

The North Esk Reservoir near Carlops was built in the mid nineteenth-century to provide a regular supply of water to the paper mills along the banks of the North Esk River. In 1905 several stone-lined graves or cists were excavated on the larger island in the reservoir. This aerial view from the 1970s is looking north east with the Kips and the Logan Valley in the top centre and Arthur's Seat just visible on the horizon. The North Esk River, shown in this Edwardian postcard, rises high in the hills above the reservoir and flows all the way through Midlothian to the Firth of Forth at Musselburgh.

Baddinsgill Reservoir was built in 1924 to supply water to Bathgate. An old drove road runs from West Linton past the reservoir and climbs to the pass at the Cauldstane Slap. The conservation village of West Linton in the Scottish Borders nestles in the shadow of the Pentlands. Amongst many local attractions is a fine moorland golf course, established in 1890, for which the Pentlands provide an attractive backdrop.

This lovely Edwardian photograph shows Mendick Hill reflected in the peaceful waters of Slipperfield Loch just south of West Linton. Reaching 1481 feet in height, Mendick Hill stands a little apart from the main range of the Pentlands. It is a very characteristic hill with extensive views on the summit and is a favourite walk for local people. Slipperfield Loch is enclosed by a thick wall of pine and fir trees, and is home to several varieties of wild birds.

The Scottish Rights of Way Society was founded in 1845 in Edinburgh to protect traditional walking routes in the Scottish hills. After a dispute in the Pentlands in the early 1880s, the Society surveyed all of the Pentland paths and negotiated with landowners to secure access rights. By 1885 the Society had erected the first signposts on most of the Pentland paths and the same year they also published the first walking guidebook to the Pentland Hills, which was titled *The Pentland Hills: Their Paths and Passes*. Copies of the guide were presented to the Edinburgh Trades Council for distribution amongst working men 'in order that healthful enjoyment and recreation afforded by rights of way across the hills should be better known'. The photograph shows the pioneering mountaineer the Reverend AE Robertson (1870-1958) at Eastside Farm road-end in 1946. Robertson was chair of the society and in 1901 became the first man to climb all of Scotland's Munros.

The Pentlands are working hills and provide a living for farmers and gamekeepers. This photograph shows heather burning on Black Law to encourage fresh growth and to recycle nutrients. Grouse depend on heather for shelter and food. They conceal their nests in longer heather and feed on the tender shoots of younger plants.

This photograph was taken around 1890 and shows a shooting party from the Garvald House estate taking part in a day's sport around Mid Hill near Dunsyre.

Wolves have been extinct in Scotland for many centuries but old wolf bones have been discovered at several sites in the Pentlands. They are remembered at Wolf Craigs on the eastern side of Craigengar. This is one of the most isolated spots in the Pentlands and the unusual rock formations add to the sense of strangeness. The Covenanters once held clandestine worship here.

On the other side of Craigengar is a meeting place of three county boundaries. In this photograph from 1975, pupils from Penicuik High School stand in Lanarkshire on the left, Peeblesshire on the right, and Midlothian at the top. From here water runs to the River Clyde and the Atlantic Ocean but on the other side of the hill water runs to the North Sea.

Above: Prominently situated at the upper end of Harperrig Reservoir in West Lothian, the ruined tower-house of Cairns Castle was built in the fifteenth century for the Crichton family of Cairns. The tower was originally L-shaped but one wing has long since disappeared. The castle was well-positioned at the end of the ancient road over the Cauldstane Slap and was a convenient hunting seat for the local nobility. Cairns Castle Coaching Inn was once a popular halt for stagecoaches on the main road between Edinburgh and Lanark. Travellers could enjoy their refreshments and also the view of the old castle and the hills beyond.

Left: The garden at Little Sparta near Dunsyre is one of the most remarkable places in the Pentlands. It was created by the artist and poet Ian Hamilton Finlay and his wife Sue Finlay, and is now recognised as an artwork of international significance. First established in 1966, the five acre garden includes concrete poetry and political aphorisms in sculptural form, combining 'avant-garden' experiments, Scottish wit and elements of the English landscape tradition. In 1983 Hamilton chose the name Little Sparta in playful response to Edinburgh's nickname as the Athens of the North, Sparta and Athens being great rivals in classical times.

Taken in 1957, this atmospheric photograph is looking towards the Cauldstane Slap, the ancient pass between the East and West Cairn Hills. This was one of the gateways through the hills for cattle drovers.

Sheep gather in the summer sunshine near Swanston. Caerketton Hill and the T Wood are in the background.